Explore!
ANCIENT EGYPTIANS

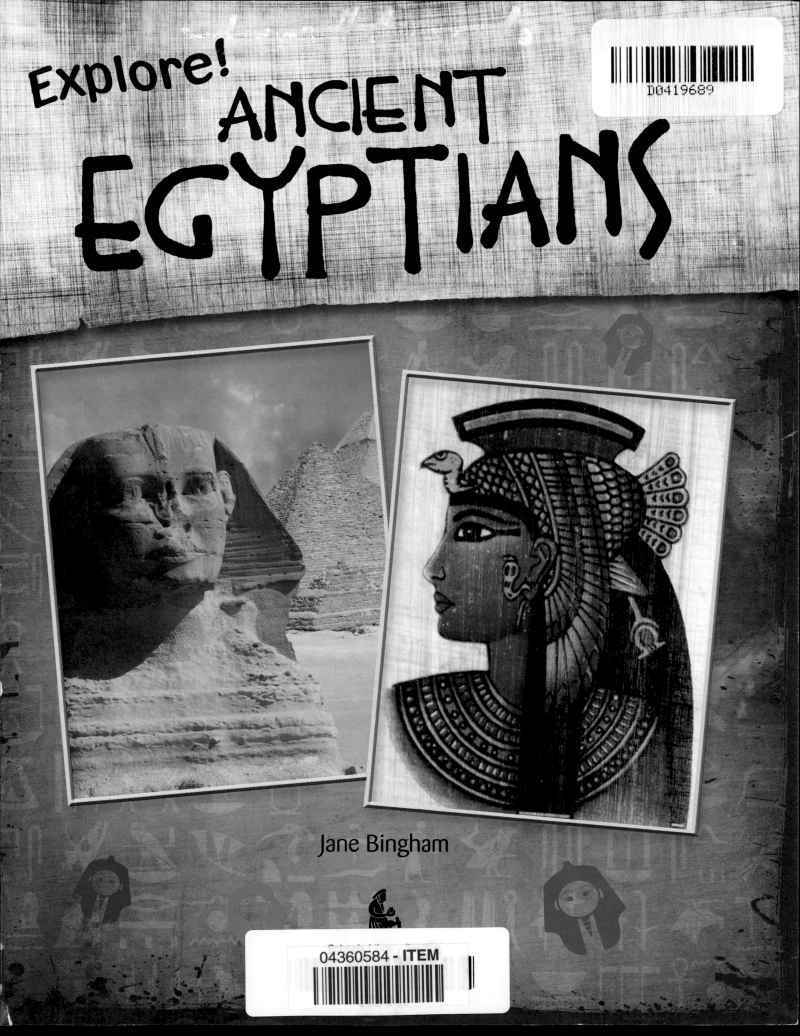

Jane Bingham

Published in 2015 by Wayland

Copyright © Wayland 2015

Wayland
338 Euston Road
London NW1 3BH

Wayland Australia
Level 17/207 Kent Street
Sydney, NSW 2000

Produced for Wayland by
White-Thomson Publishing
www.wtpub.co.uk
+44 (0)843 208 7460

Editor: Jane Bingham
Designer: Elaine Wilkinson
Picture researcher: Jane Bingham
Illustrations for step-by-step and map p.10:
Stefan Chabluk
Map p.6: Wayland
Proof reader: Lucy Ross

First published in 2014 by Wayland

A cataloguing record for this title is available
from the British Library.

ISBN 978 0 7502 8886 6

Dewey Number 932-dc23

Printed in China

Wayland is a division of Hachette Children's
Books, an Hachette UK company
www.hachette.co.uk

Picture acknowledgements:
The author and publisher would like to thank the
following agencies and people for allowing these
pictures to be reproduced:
Cover (top left) Morgan Rauscher/Shutterstock;
(top right) Jose Ignacio Soto/Shutterstock;
(bottom left) Nico Traut/Shutterstock; (bottom
right) piotrwzk/Shutterstock; p.1(left) Pius
Lee/Shutterstock; (right) Ashwin Kharidehal
Abhirama/Dreamstime; p.3 Patryk Kosminder/
Shutterstock; p.4 Pius Lee/Shutterstock; p.5
(top) Airphoto/Dreamstime; (bottom) leoks/
Shutterstock; p.7 (top) meunierd/Shutterstock;
(bottom) Wikimedia; p.8 Patryk Kosminder/
Shutterstock; p.9 (top) mountainpix/Shutterstock;
(bottom) Ashwin Kharidehal Abhirama/
Dreamstime; p.11 (top) Empire331/Dreamstime;
p.12 (left) Tanya Borozenets/Dreamstime; (right)
Indos82/Dreamstime; p.13 (top) Wikimedia;
(bottom) Wikimedia; p.14 Charles & Josette
Lenars/Corbis; p.15 (top) Louvre, Paris/Peter
Willi/The Bridgeman Library; (bottom) Francis
G. Mayer/Corbis; p.16 Werner Forman/Werner
Forman/Corbis; p.17 (top) Berenike/istock;
(bottom) Wikimedia; p.18 Wikimedia; p.19 (top)
Wikimedia; (bottom) Wikimedia; p.20 Wikimedia;
p.22 Wikimedia; p.23 (top) Icon72/Dreamstime;
(bottom) Wikimedia; p.24 Wikimedia; p.25 (top)
Wikimedia; (bottom) Netfalls-Reemy Musser/
Shutterstock; p.26 PRILL/Shutterstock; p.27
(top) Wikimedia; (bottom) Fedor Selivanov/
Shutterstock; p.28 (top) Nickolay Vinokurov/
Shutterstock; (bottom) Christian Musat/
Shutterstock; p.29 (top) leoks/Shutterstock;
(middle) Fedor Selivanov/Shutterstock; (bottom)
mountainpix/ Fedor Selivanov/Shutterstock; p.31
Wikimedia.

Contents

Who were the ancient Egyptians?

The ancient Egyptian people lived along the banks of the River Nile in North Africa. They created an astonishing civilization that lasted for over 3,000 years, from around 3100BCE to 30BCE.

Gods and pharaohs

Religion was at the heart of Egyptian life. People worshipped many different gods and goddesses. Even their rulers, the pharaohs, were treated as gods! Massive temples were built in honour of the gods, and pharaohs were buried in gigantic tombs.

The pyramids and the Sphinx at Giza were built more than four thousand years ago. The pyramids were tombs for pharaohs. The Sphinx has a lion's body and a pharaoh's head.

These tomb paintings show Egyptian priests dressed as gods. The figures are surrounded by hieroglyphs (picture symbols).

Life after death

The Egyptians believed in life after death. They thought that people would need their bodies in the next world, so they preserved them as mummies. The dead were also buried with their possessions. Mummies of pharaohs were placed in golden coffins surrounded by their treasures. Less wealthy people had painted wooden coffins and were often buried with useful items, such as tools. Some tombs contained wooden models, like a herd of cows, to represent the dead person's possessions.

How do we know?

Archaeologists have uncovered amazing evidence about the ancient Egyptians. Many buildings and statues have survived, and a range of remarkable objects have been found in tombs. The Egyptians recorded their history in paintings and carvings, and in a form of picture-writing, called hieroglyphics. All this evidence has helped to build up a picture of life in ancient Egypt.

This golden burial mask comes from the tomb of the young pharaoh, Tutankhamun. It was discovered in the 1920s when archaeologists excavated his tomb.

Early kingdoms

People began to settle on the banks of the River Nile around 5000BCE. They lived in small communities, fishing in the river, growing crops and keeping animals. Some farming villages grew into trading towns and by 3500BCE there were two successful kingdoms: Upper Egypt in the south, and Lower Egypt in the north.

Egypt unites

The two Egyptian kingdoms remained separate until around 3100BCE, when King Menes of Upper Egypt defeated the ruler of Lower Egypt. He united the two kingdoms, creating a capital city called Memphis. Menes was followed by a series of powerful kings who ruled from Memphis for the next 3,000 years.

A map of ancient Egypt showing the main cities, with modern names in brackets.

The Old Kingdom

Around 2650BCE, a new stage in Egypt's history began. Later known as the Old Kingdom, it lasted for about 500 years and was a time of great wealth. During this period, the Egyptian kings started building giant pyramids. The most famous monuments of the Old Kingdom are the Great Pyramid and the Sphinx at Giza (see page 4).

The step pyramid at Saqqara, near Memphis, was the first Egyptian pyramid. It was built for Pharaoh Dhoser around the year 2620BCE.

A portrait of Pharaoh Mentuhotep, a Middle Kingdom ruler. The early Egyptian rulers wore very tall crowns.

The Middle Kingdom

After the collapse of the Old Kingdom in 2150BCE, there was a time of chaos when different groups struggled to gain power. Then, in 1975BCE, a new family of rulers brought peace and order to Egypt. This was the start of the Middle Kingdom, which lasted for the next 300 years. In this period, the Egyptians gained new lands in the south, and art and writing flourished. The Middle Kingdom ended around 1640BCE when Egypt was invaded by the warlike Hyskos people from Asia.

A mighty power

The Hyskos people ruled northern Egypt until 1552 BCE, when kings from Thebes gained control of all the Egyptian lands. This marked the start of the New Kingdom, that lasted for nearly 500 years.

The enormous temples at Karnak were built by pharaohs of the New Kingdom.

Power and wealth

The pharaohs of the New Kingdom gained a large empire and became very rich. Some of their wealth was used to pay for massive building projects, including a huge set of temples at Karnak, and a burial site for the pharaohs, known as the Valley of the Kings.

Great rulers

Some New Kingdom rulers were especially successful. Pharaoh Tutmosis III led his army in 17 campaigns, and the Egyptian Empire reached its largest size during his reign. Ramesses II reigned for 67 years. He defended Egypt from enemy forces and paid for many impressive temples and monuments.

One of the most outstanding rulers was a woman. At first Queen Hatshepsut ruled on behalf of her young nephew, but she was soon recognized as a pharaoh in her own right. She commanded the Egyptian Army, encouraged trade and organized building projects.

Queen Hatshepsut dressed like a male pharaoh, and even wore a false beard!

Losing power

After the death of Ramesses II, the New Kingdom gradually weakened, until it came to an end in 1069BCE. Over the next 700 years, Egypt was ruled by Libyans, Nubians, Assyrians and Persians, although there were brief periods of independence.

In 332BCE, Alexander the Great led a Greek Army in an invasion of Egypt and founded a new capital at Alexandria. After his death, Egypt was ruled by pharaohs from the Greek Ptolemy family. The last Ptolemy ruler was Queen Cleopatra. During her reign Egypt was conquered by the Romans and became part of the Roman Empire.

Queen Cleopatra was the last Egyptian pharaoh. She was famous for her beauty.

The Egyptian world

The ancient Egyptians dominated the lands around the eastern Mediterranean Sea. For centuries they traded with neighbouring countries, and at the time of the New Kingdom they controlled an empire that stretched from Nubia in the south to northern Syria.

Trade

Egypt was at the centre of a network of trade routes that ran between Africa and the Mediterranean Sea. The Egyptians imported gold and ivory from Nubia. Copper, timber and horses came from the lands of the Near East (present-day Lebanon and Syria), and wine, oil and silver were imported from Greece. In exchange for these valuable items, Egypt exported grain, wine, linen and papyrus (a kind of paper made from reeds), as well as many fine craft goods.

A map of the Egyptian Empire around 1440BCE. The lands coloured pink were ruled by the Egyptians.

Tribute

During the time of the New Kingdom, the pharaohs demanded tribute from all the lands in their Empire. This meant that all the conquered countries had to give the pharaoh the best of their trading goods. Tribute goods flowed into Egypt and the pharaohs became incredibly rich.

The Egyptians used large sailing ships to travel down rivers and cross seas. Their ships were equipped with oars and a steering paddle.

These model soldiers were found inside a tomb. They show the Egyptian Army as a highly disciplined group of fighting men. The Army played an important role in the Empire, conquering new lands and keeping order.

Keeping control

The pharaoh was in charge of running Egypt, and was helped in this task by three ministers. Two men called viziers were responsible for Upper and Lower Egypt, while a viceroy governed Nubia. These three men had a large staff of officials who collected taxes, ran the law courts and supervised building and faming projects. Priests also collected some taxes for the pharaoh. Taxes were paid in the form of goods or labour, so they needed a lot of organizing.

Religion and beliefs

The people of Ancient Egypt worshipped many gods. Huge temples were built on the banks of the River Nile and each village had its own shrine, where people went to say prayers and leave offerings.

Gods and goddesses

One of the most important gods was Re, the god of the sun. He was the father of Isis, the goddess of motherhood, and Osiris, the god of the underworld. Other leading gods were Ma'at, the goddess of truth, and the falcon-headed Horus, who was seen as the chief protector of Egypt. The healing goddess Bast took the shape of a cat and Sobek, the god of the Nile, looked like a crocodile.

Isis wears a crown showing the sun held in the horns of a cow. A serpent hovers over her head.

Osiris looks like a pharaoh. He holds the pharaohs' symbols of power - a shepherd's crook and a flail (whip).

Priests and priestesses

Priests made offerings to statues of the gods. On special feast days they led public processions and sacrificed animals to please the gods. Most of the priests were men, but a few women worked as priestesses or as temple dancers and musicians. Ordinary people were not allowed inside the temples.

A statue of a priest. Priests had their heads shaved as a sign that they were pure beings.

A statue of Bast, the cat goddess. Cats were seen as sacred animals, and their bodies were often preserved as mummies.

Talking to the gods

The Egyptian people tried to follow the will of the gods. If they needed to make a big decision, they paid a scribe to write down their question for the god. Their request was handed to a priest who went inside the temple and returned with an answer. In return for this guidance, people made generous offerings to the god.

Everyday life

Pharaohs lived in huge stone palaces, but ordinary Egyptian homes were built from river mud. Rich Egyptians had large, comfortable villas with a central hall for entertaining guests. Poorer families were crowded into small, bare homes.

This tomb painting shows an Egyptian farmer ploughing his fields while his wife sows seeds.

All kinds of jobs

Most Egyptian men farmed the land and fished in the River Nile. Some were bakers, brewers or weavers, while others worked as merchants or joined the Army. Skilled craftworkers produced a wide range of goods, including weapons, pots, jewellery and furniture. Educated men had jobs as government officials, priests, scribes and doctors.

Women and children

Egyptian women were expected to run the family home. The rich had servants to do the cooking and cleaning, while poorer women did their own housework, with the help of their daughters. Women did not usually have jobs of their own, but some helped their husbands in their work.

Most boys and girls did not go to school. Instead, boys trained to do the same work as their fathers and girls prepared for life as a wife and mother. Young children played with wooden balls, dolls and spinning tops, and some had model animals to pull along the ground.

An Egyptian family group. Most families were much larger than this and it was not unusual for a couple to have as many as ten children!

Servants and slaves

In early Egyptian times, rich people had servants to help them run their homes. But once the Egyptians began to conquer new lands, they captured prisoners-of-war and used them as slaves. Slaves had no freedom and had to obey their masters at all times. Some had a very hard life, quarrying stone, and building temples, palaces and tombs.

This sculpture shows a Nubian prisoner-of-war. Prisoners captured in battle were used as slaves.

A day in a temple school

Most Egyptian children did not go to school. The sons and daughters of pharaohs had personal tutors, while poorer children stayed at home to help their parents. However, some boys attended a temple school where they were taught by priests. This fictional diary entry describes a day in a temple school.

Early in the morning I meet up with my friends in the temple courtyard, ready for another day at school.

We sit cross-legged on the ground and listen to our teacher, one of the temple priests. We have to get used to working like this because it's the way the scribes sit to do their work. Even the youngest pupils, who are just five years old, are expected to work really hard. If we make a mistake, our teacher will beat us!

Most of our day is spent reading and writing. First we read a text out loud, then we copy out what we have read. We write with a reed pen dipped in black or red ink, using flakes of stone that can be thrown away at the end of the day. It is very important to learn to write perfectly because one day we will use papyrus, which is very expensive to make.

Once we have learned to read and write really well, most of us will leave school and find work as a scribe. There is plenty of work for scribes, composing letters and legal documents or working in a temple.

A few pupils will stay on at school and study other subjects, such as mathematics, religion and engineering. Father hopes I will study for many years and become a great architect!

The diary entry on these pages has been written for this book. Can you create your own diary entry for a boy or girl living in an Egyptian pharaoh's palace? Use the facts in this book and in other sources to help you write about a day in their life.

Feasting and fun

People in Ancient Egypt found plenty of ways to enjoy their leisure time. Wealthy Egyptians held lively parties with feasting, music and dancing. Rich young men went out hunting and people of all classes played sports and games.

Parties

Pharaohs and nobles held elaborate feasts with lots of meat, fruit and vegetables to eat and wine and beer to drink. Guests relaxed on low seats or cushions and listened to musicians as they ate. Later in the evening, there was more entertainment from singers, storytellers, dancers, jugglers and acrobats.

This painting shows guests at a feast with cones of perfumed fat on their heads. During the evening, the fat slowly melted, keeping the guests cool and sweet-smelling!

Hunting

Poor Egyptians went hunting for food, but pharaohs and nobles hunted purely for sport. Sometimes they hunted river birds, using a curved throwing-stick to bring down their prey. Sometimes they rode their chariots into the desert, chasing after lions, ostriches and cobras. One of the most dangerous sports was hunting hippos. The hunters formed a team to spear the hippo and catch it in a net.

A nobleman hunting birds from a boat on the River Nile.

Sports and games

The Egyptians competed against each other in gymnastics, running, rowing, jumping and throwing the javelin. They played a kind of hockey, using palm-tree branches as sticks, and they had tugs-of-war, in which each team pulled as hard as they could on a rope. People of all classes liked to relax at home by playing board games. One of the most popular games was senet, which was played by moving pieces on a narrow board (see page 20).

This Egyptian game was played on a board shaped like a hippopotamus, and players moved tall wooden pegs around the board. Sadly, the hippo's head has been damaged.

Play the game of senet

In the Egyptian game of senet, two players threw coloured sticks to show how many places they could move their counters around a board. You can try a simple version of senet, using a home-made board, modern counters and a dice. See if you can beat a friend at this ancient game of skill and chance!

You will need:

piece of card measuring 20 cm x 6 cm

ruler

pencil

dice

14 counters (7 for each player)
Hint: You can make counters from card – make two sets of seven in contrasting colours.

Several senet boards have been found in Egyptian tombs. They all look slightly different, but archaeologists have managed to work out how the game was played.

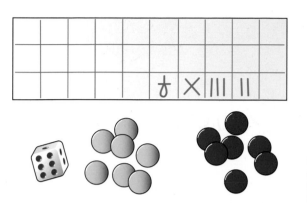

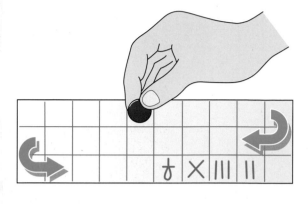

1

First, mark out a senet board on your card. It should have 30 squares (three rows of ten), each measuring 2 cm square. Then draw picture symbols on four squares, as shown above. The cross indicates the 'danger square'. The other three symbols show 'safe squares'.

2

Players start in the top left square and end at the bottom right. They move their counters along the board in a reversed letter 'S'. The game begins with the first player throwing a dice and moving her counter that number of squares along the board.

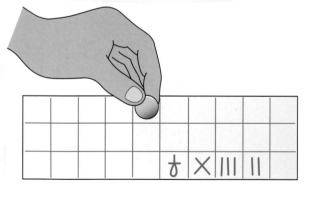

3

Once the first player has moved, it is the turn of the second player. If he lands on his opponent's counter, he can take its place. He removes his opponent's counter from the board and the first player has to start all over again.

4

You can start a new counter any time. The winner is the first player to get all seven of their counters to the bottom right-hand corner of the board. This is not as easy as it seems because you must follow the rules below:

1. You cannot land on one of your own pieces. Instead, you have to miss a go.

2. You cannot switch with your opponent's counter if she has two or more pieces in a row.

3. You cannot switch with your opponent if she is on a 'safe' square. (But if your opponent is on the 'danger square', it's fine to switch with her!)

Pyramids and temples

How did the Egyptians manage to build their enormous temples and pyramids without the help of any four-wheeled vehicles or lifting equipment? Archaeologists have made a careful study of buildings and records in order to work out how it was done.

Pharaoh Khufu's Great Pyramid is on the left. It has lost its smooth limestone covering, but some remains of the casing can be seen on Pharaoh Khafre's pyramid on the right.

Building the Great Pyramid

Pharaoh Khufu built his Great Pyramid around 2550BCE. It was constructed from over two million blocks of limestone that were quarried from rocks in the desert. Teams of builders transported the blocks across the desert by attaching them to ropes and dragging them over rollers placed on the ground. The pyramid was constructed one layer at a time and a large ramp was built against one of its sides, so the builders could pull the stones up to the next level. Once it was completed, the walls of the pyramid were covered with large limestone slabs, creating a smooth, four-sided structure.

The temple of Pharaoh Hatshepsut near Luxor was carved from the side of a cliff!

Building temples

Tall stone temples were built by filling up their centre with sand and rubble. This temporary filling supported the structure, and gave the builders somewhere to stand while they put the stones in place. When the structure was finished, all the sand and rubble was removed, leaving the stone temple, ready for carving and decoration.

Architects

Designing pyramids and temples was a highly skilled job and Egyptian architects were greatly respected. The most famous architect in Ancient Egypt was Imhotep, who designed the first pyramid. Imhotep was also a priest, a doctor, an astronomer and an adviser to Pharaoh Dhoser. After his death he was worshipped as a god.

A statue of the architect Imhotep.

Medicine, science and magic

Egyptian doctors were famous throughout the Middle East for their skill and knowledge. They studied medical texts and trained for several years, often specializing in a part of the body, such as the stomach or the eyes.

An Egyptian charm showing Thoth, one of the gods of healing. People wore charms like this to keep disease away.

Knowledge and belief

Doctors did not understand very much about how the human body worked. For example, they believed that water and air passed through the heart! However, they were experts at setting broken bones and sewing up cuts. They made medicines from plants and minerals, and used honey to help heal wounds. If their methods did not work, doctors turned to religion and magic. They said prayers and used spells and magic charms to help cure their patients.

The brains and internal organs of a dead body were stored in canopic jars. The lids of these jars show Egyptian gods.

Embalming

One area where science and religion combined was embalming. Egyptians believed that they would need their bodies in the next world. This meant that the dead bodies had to be embalmed (preserved). The embalming process took 70 days, and at the end of this time a mummy was created.

Making mummies

The process of making a mummy had several stages. First, the embalmers removed the brains and the internal organs. Then they covered the body with a salt called natron to help dry it out. When the body was completely dry, it was stuffed with linen soaked in oil and resin (a kind of sticky sap from plants). Lastly, the embalmers wrapped the body in layers of bandages, creating a mummy. This was placed in a decorated coffin with a portrait of the dead person on its lid.

This decorated wooden coffin would have contained a mummified body.

Art, music and writing

Art was an essential part of ancient Egyptian life. Palaces, temples and tombs were covered with paintings and carvings. Objects of all kinds – from pots to coffins – were decorated with colourful images.

Egyptian style

The Egyptians did not aim to create realistic scenes. Instead, they often showed humans and gods in a stylized way, with the shoulders facing the front, but the head drawn from the side. This style of painting meant that a god like Horus could be easily recognized by his falcon's head.

A carved and painted scene showing a pharaoh offering gifts to Horus.

Musicians

Men and women worked as musicians in ancient Egypt. They played in temples, entertained guests at feasts and marched to war with soldiers. There is evidence that musicians played harps, lyres, flutes, trumpets, drums, rattles, castanets and bells. Sometimes they clapped their hands and sang as part of their performance.

This painting shows a temple musician playing a harp. You can also see the hand of a second musician holding a set of bells.

Scribes

Egyptian scribes recorded the history of their people using hieroglyphs (picture symbols). They often wrote on papyrus, but hieroglyphs were also painted on walls and carved in stone. Hieroglyphs were a mystery to the early explorers of ancient Egypt, until the Rosetta Stone was found in 1798. It had a Greek translation beside an Egyptian text, which unlocked the secret of the Egyptian symbols. Thanks to this discovery, historians have been able to learn an enormous amount about the history of Egypt and the lives of its people.

The Egyptians believed that their hieroglyphs had magic powers and could even come to life.

Facts and figures

The Great Pyramid at Giza (also called Khufu's Pyramid) is 146 metres (481 feet) high. Until the nineteenth century it was the tallest building in the world.

Many people believe the pyramids were built by slaves. In fact, they were the work of teams of skilled builders. One team called themselves the 'Friends of Khufu'.

The people of ancient Egypt were one of the first civilizations to keep household pets. Cats, dogs, hawks, ibises and monkeys were common family pets.

Each side of the Great Pyramid measures 230 metres (755 feet) at its base. The four sides are perfectly in line with the four points of the compass (north, south, east and west).

Egyptian doctors believed that people thought with their hearts. They did not consider the brain to be a very useful organ.

The male pharaohs never let their hair be seen. They always wore a crown or a headdress called a *nemes*.

There are more than 700 hieroglyphs. Many of the symbols stand for an object, but some represent a sound. This makes Egyptian text very hard to read!

Both men and women wore eye make-up in ancient Egypt. It was usually green (made from copper) or black (made from lead). People used eye-paint as protection from the sun and believed it had healing powers.

Glossary

archaeologist Someone who learns about the past by digging up old objects and buildings.

astronomer Someone who studies the moon, sun and stars.

BCE The letters BCE stand for 'before common era'. They refer to dates before the birth of Christ.

campaign A series of actions by an army intended to achieve a goal.

canopic jar A container for storing the brains and internal organs of a dead body.

civilization A well-organized society.

embalmer Someone who prepares a body for burial.

evidence Facts and information about something.

excavate To dig up or uncover.

fictional Made-up or invented.

hieroglyph A symbol used in picture-writing.

hieroglyphics Picture-writing.

javelin A light spear thrown in a competitive sport.

mineral A rock or other substance found in the earth. Diamonds and salt are both minerals.

monument A statue or building put up in memory of a person or event.

mummy A dead body that has been preserved and wrapped in bandages.

next world A place where ancient Egyptians believed that people went after death.

opponents People who are on opposite sides in a game, sport or war.

papyrus A form of paper made from reeds.

quarry To dig stone out of a pit or a cliff.

reed pen A pen made from the stem of a water reed.

scribe Someone who writes out documents or records.

senet An ancient Egyptian board game.

shrine A place or a building where people offer gifts and prayers to gods.

underworld A place under the earth, where ancient Egyptians believed people went after death.

Further reading

Ancient Egyptians (Craft Box),
Jillian Powell (Wayland, 2013)

The Egyptians (History from Objects),
John Malam (Wayland,2012)

Ancient Egyptians (Hail!),
Jen Green (Wayland, 2013)

The Egyptians (The Gruesome Truth
About), Jillian Powell (Wayland, 2010)

Websites

http://www.ancientegypt.co.uk/
A beautifully illustrated site by The British Museum. It includes sections on gods and goddesses,
mummies and pharaohs. The sections include objects to explore and challenges to try.

http://www.bbc.co.uk/history/ancient/egyptians/
A BBC website written by subject experts. It includes an interactive game on the skill
of embalming.

http://www.childrensuniversity.manchester.ac.uk/interactives/history/egypt/
A site for children produced by the University of Manchester. It offers a journey through
Egyptian history and has features on hieroglyphics and numbers.

http://video.nationalgeographic.com.au/video/kids/people-places-kids/egypt-tombs-kids/
A video tour of the pyramids, produced by *National Geographic Magazine.*

Index